The Three du Maurier Sisters

Daphne, Angela & Jeanne

Michael Williams

British Library Cataloguing in Publication Data.
A catalogue record for this book is available from the British Library.

ISBN 978-0-9570481-1-9

Published by
Polperro Heritage Press,
Clifton-upon-Teme, Worcestershire
WR6 6EN
United Kingdom
www.polperropress.co.uk

Printed in Great Britain by
Orphans Press, Leominster
United Kingdom

The three du Maurier sisters on Hampstead Heath, 1918, from a painting by Frederick Whiting.
Left to right: Daphne, Jeanne and Angela.

ACKNOWLEDGMENTS

I am deeply indebted to Christian Browning for his generosity in providing evocative family photographs, including the beautiful cover shot of his mother and two aunts which comes from The Chichester Partnership. He also kindly gave me an interview at Ferryside and read the manuscript. I cannot begin to thank Christian enough for his warm co-operation.

Ann Willmore of Bookends, Fowey, has been a source of knowledge and encouragement from the idea stage. While my wife Sonia and Elaine Beckton have once more been invaluable allies and I am grateful to Dr A. L. Rowse who long ago said 'Quote anything of mine, provided you let the reader know it's mine'. His reference to the rich du Maurier ancestry is a paragraph from *Friends and Contemporaries* (1989). And, of course, nobody can write about Dame Daphne and her family without giving the smartest salutes to Margaret Forster whose biography *Daphne du Maurier* is an impressive granite tor volume.

As an old regional publisher, I have special thanks for Jeremy Johns of Polperro Heritage Press: his skill and gentlemanly guidance. And last and most importantly, the three sisters. What a trio.

INTRODUCTION

The three du Maurier sisters: Daphne, Angela and Jeanne.

They all looked completely feminine but they should perhaps have been brothers. Someone, who knew them well, reckoned 'They would have made energetic boys.'

My late stepson Richard had three daughters and looking at them I sometimes think of the du Maurier sisters. Various talents and natural rivalries. Kindred spirits, yet individuality. Richard's fourth child, a son, doing well in the film business as I write. Gerald du Maurier longed for a son and Daphne was his favourite and middle daughter.

Angela was the oldest, born in 1904, but Daphne was the most famous: two writers. Jeanne was the youngest, a painter.

Dame Daphne may not have been Cornish but she was one of the greatest writers to have come out of Cornwall: that rare character, a bestseller who defied classification. Critics calling her 'a romantic novelist' were wide of the mark, her most successful novel *Rebecca* capturing readers' imaginations in a way that few other twentieth century novels matched.

Her long short story *The Birds* was turned into Hitchcock horror for the cinema screen and her factual *Vanishing Cornwall* should be required reading for all planning officers, a writer for all seasons.

The Birds, in fact, grew out of a ploughing scene at Menabilly Barton, gulls swooping, circling round the farmer's head. In a flash, she wondered 'What if those birds attacked?'

The du Maurier ancestry is intriguing. Dr AL Rowse, writing of Daphne, reflected: 'The historian is naturally fascinated by her fabulous historical background, the brilliant gifted and variegated Anglo-French family from which she comes. Every good fairy seems to have stood at her christening, including the clergyman who performed the ceremony – a Reverend Bernard Shaw.'

There was the girls' great-great grandmother Mary Anne Clarke, mistress of the Duke of York, and the considerable influence of their father Sir Gerald du Maurier, eminent actor-manager of Wyndham's Theatre. Their childhoods were glamorous and coincided with Gerald's top successes.

Angela, on the surface, was the most conventional of the three though, now and then, in conversation and in her authorship, you detected a whiff of the Bohemian. A great traveller, who was reputed to have as many friends as the night has stars: people like Cecil Beaton and Gladys Cooper. She was the only one of the three to follow in her father's footsteps and act on the stage, and throughout her long life Angela remained loyal to the high Anglican faith, at ease in the ritual.

Jeanne du Maurier is arguably the underestimated sister, her painting embracing still life, landscape and flowers and occasionally a portrait. A pianist too with a liking for Bach and Mozart, Ravel and Chopin, Jeanne rode horses and kept canaries and, in her youth, she enjoyed tennis and hockey. She became a Roman Catholic, saying she was simply returning to the beliefs of her forebears. While Daphne was the only sister to build her own chapel, in the basement of her final Cornish home Kilmarth.

I had the good fortune to know all three sisters – acquaintances, rather than friends. Though Daphne was an influence and inspiration and gave good sound advice during my early years as a regional publisher.

They each had an inner mechanism which is not easily defined, that mechanism somehow setting them apart. Without showing off in any way, there was a hint of theatricality – moments when they might have stepped out of a West End production by their father.

There was no suggestion of acting: they simply stood out, different like the Foots, another Westcountry dynasty, and the Leaches yet another creative family producing quality pottery.

The relationship between Daphne and her elder sister was especially close: Angela frequently confiding in Daphne about her "pashes." And they refrained from criticising one another. Angela too understood her sister needed to be alone, while Daphne was aware of Angela's need to have circles of friends. Margaret Forster though expressed the view that in the 20s and 30s Foy Quiller-Couch was 'the person she (Daphne) was closest to...' It's no coincidence then that some of her novels and short stories explore the contrasting themes of sociability and solitude.

What would Jeanne have made of her sisters as portrait subjects? The character, the blue eyes and beauty in Daphne's face? Or an action portrait of the novelist, not working at her desk but her swinging stride on a walk with her dogs? And Angela? There is a stunning studio shot of her by Anthony Buckley, of London: the back cover for the 1963 edition of her Irish novel *The Road to Leenane*. Surely something like that: eyes mirroring an unasked or unanswered question. Or if Angela insisted on Ferryside, then there watching river life would be fine. The actress is there always. But would she have the time to pose? 'I've only two minutes,' was a frequent comment.

And what would Jeanne have made of a self-portrait? I suspect she would have said 'No, thank you.' She would have preferred a portrait by her mentor and friend Dod Proctor.

All three du Maurier sisters developed along different routes, the influence of their father Gerald never far away. In the eye of imagination, we can picture them talking over afternoon tea or perhaps Angela enjoying a Cinzano: the conversation witty and wise, occasionally Bohemian. Daphne spoke with a slight beguiling lisp, a lovely voice on radio. Jeanne had a quite different voice, like the River Fowey flowing gently in the upper part of the Fowey Valley, just below Jamaica Inn. I heard Angela speak at a meeting. Her command of language, her ability to argue her case and hold the attention of her audience had the hallmarks of a Member of Parliament.

Writing about them is a pleasure and a challenge. I like to think their spirits may be with us on this Cornwall-Dartmoor journey.

Let us head for Menabilly and hope it's high tide.

Menabilly, the Rashleigh mansion and Daphne's home for many years. In 1824 William Rashleigh of Menabilly had alterations made. These included masons demolishing the buttress against the north-west corner of the house. In a small room or cell, they found the skeleton of a young man dressed in the clothes of a Cavalier, as worn during the Civil War. On Mr Rashleigh's orders he was buried 'with great reverence' in Tywardreath churchyard. The owner later learned members of the Grenville family had hidden at Menabilly before the rising of 1648. Today Menabilly is strictly private and not open to the public.

Daphne du Maurier was professional and prolific - and a biographer's dream. Not until her parents bought their house by the Bodinnic-Fowey ferry crossing did she begin to find herself as a person and the deep pleasure of solitude, Cornwall, in a way, becoming the window of her writing. 'du Maurier is able to view the whole of Cornwall as a bird would, but also walk along the ground and experience that same world in detail... Landscape is key to the concept of ancient Cornwall put forward in Jamaica Inn and du Maurier uses it to create an atmosphere of mystery and foreboding in her Gothic tale'. That was the assessment of Dr Gemma Goodman of the University of Warwick in her thesis on Daphne and Jack Clemo, the china clay country poet and author. And interestingly Daphne herself said standing in a field on the edge of Bodmin Moor she felt like 'an astronaut in time'.

DAPHNE

Daphne had a deep love of the sea and it was at high tide that her stories invariably began.

Menabilly, seat of the Rashleighs and her home for more than a quarter of a century, was the great passion of her life pouring energy and fantasy into it. Three miles from Fowey, Menabilly is a property which has you searching for adjectives.

Daphne told me she first came across the name in an old guidebook. She was determined to see it. Locals warned: 'The house is all shut up and the owner lives in Devon. The drive is about three miles long and overgrown.'

But trespass she did and she later wrote an essay in *Countryside Character*, published in 1946. It was the moment of discovery: 'I edged my way on to the lawn, and there she stood. My house of secrets. My elusive Menabilly...'

When I once asked her about its influence on her writing, she replied 'Menabilly and I are one...'

And it is interesting to reflect when someone tackled Alfred Hitchcock about *Rebecca* he said 'A story about two wives, one alive, the other dead, and a house and the house is the strongest character.'

The strength and success of *Rebecca* surprised Daphne.

Probably the most read Gothic novel, it has scored in six art forms: novel, film, play, opera, musical and television series – and it has spawned two follow-up titles, both hugely readable. First, *Mrs de Winter* by Susan Hill in 1993 and in 2001 *Rebecca's Tale* by Sally Beauman whom I had the privilege of meeting at the du Maurier Festival in Fowey. Sally opening her first chapter with 'Last night I dreamt I went to Manderley again. These dreams are now recurring with a puzzling frequency, and I've come to dread them.'

Though Manderley is based – to a degree – on Menabilly, Daphne started working on it, drafts in a notebook, late 1937 when her husband Boy Browning was commanding officer of the Second Battalion, Grenadier Guards in Alexandria. She later confessed she had to attend certain cocktail parties but all she wanted to do was write this novel set in Cornwall.

Notebooks and the first few chapters were put aside until their return to England some months later. Daphne calculated she completed the manuscript in about four months making some changes. The husband Henry now became Maxim: Henry too dull she thought. In due course she sent it off to her publisher Victor Gollancz wondering if it was 'overdone.'

Fortunately for all of us du Maurier fans, he liked the work – the rest is on-going publishing history.

Why?

Rebecca is arguably one of the most menacing books ever written, almost a nightmare in flashback. Hitchcock's classic film was, of course, a terrific boost: the backdrops gorgeous. The contrast in the two wives: Rebecca beautiful and adulterous. The timid, nameless second wife, her fear of Mrs Danvers and Rebecca's ghost have us turning the pages or watching the screen with a curious cocktail of anxiety and anticipation. And Emilia Fox baring her breast in the latest TV version gives a new frisson. While Mrs Danvers in any medium remains the housekeeper from hell.

A postscript to *Rebecca* is that, over the years, I heard from more than one source in and around Fowey that a factor in its writing was an element of jealousy. Tommy Browning's earlier fiancé was a woman called Jan Ricardo and Daphne harboured the suspicion her husband found the glamorous Jan more attractive. The facts are the dark-haired rival (in Daphne's mind) married in 1937 and died during the war, throwing herself under a train.

In her Menabilly years Daphne did her writing in a garden hut which she had erected in the grounds. She lived simply and quietly: swimming, walking and reading. You got the impression she absorbed atmosphere like a sponge.

One day I asked her which title was her favourite. 'Each book has given me pleasure,' she said, 'but you know when it's completed the whole thing fades. Each has its phase.' In our interview in the 1960s she explained 'I work to a regular pattern, writing from 10.30am to 1.30pm and from 5.30pm to 7.30pm. Occasionally I work in the afternoon but, weather permitting, I like to walk the dogs. When writing, there's always a dictionary nearby; I write rapidly... all my books have been finished inside twelve months.'

Robert Louis Stevenson, the author of *Treasure Island*, was one of her acknowledged masters, a Scot who also wrote poetry. This is perhaps the place in which to say how poets and their creativity inspired her. She was intrigued by the sound of words and the rhythm of good writing. Collin Langley has put together two impressive manuscripts (housed in Exeter University for research purposes) *Daphne du Maurier: The Appeal of Poet and Poetry*. Both beautifully illustrated by her son Christian 'Kits' Browning, the photographs capturing more than mood, images with heart and soul.

Collin Langley in his *Conclusion: The Mutuality of Poetry and Prose* observes 'So did poetry influence Daphne's prose? I looked beyond her renowned imagery and description of nature. I found in her sentences considerable sound-coupling and repetition of words both used to telling but different effect. Adjacent words with similar sound smooth a passage of prose but the technique of repetition emphasises or adds drama; for example the confrontation scene between *Rebecca*'s Mrs de Winter and Danvers.'

And we must not forget Daphne's own poetry published in *The Rebecca Notebook* and *Other Memories* and *Myself When Young*. There is a moving poem written whilst a patient at The Duchy Hospital, Truro. I mentioned this to Kits and he replied that she wrote it when the shadow of her writer's block had fallen.

Daphne's published letters to Oriel Malet, correspondence full of insight, showed her and Kit's enthusiasm for making short television films. Notably as devotees of W. B. Yeats's poetry they collaborated on a film in 1965 entitled *The Last Romantic*, marking the Irish poet's centenary. Daphne provided the script, Kits directing and producing, with Cyril Cussack, that superb Irish actor, narrating. It was broadcast on Irish TV in about 1965 and later distributed by CBS worldwide.

* * *

Over the centuries layer upon layer of history and tales have grown in the Cornish countryside and along its jagged coastline, events leaving 'atmosphere'. Dame Daphne has probably pinned Cornwall's past to paper more vividly than any other writer of fiction. But, of course, her themes were not confined to Cornwall. The Scapegoat, *for example, was set in France and* Not After Midnight, *five long stories, relate to Venice and Crete, Ireland and Jerusalem, and East Anglia, settings as contrasting as her plots.*

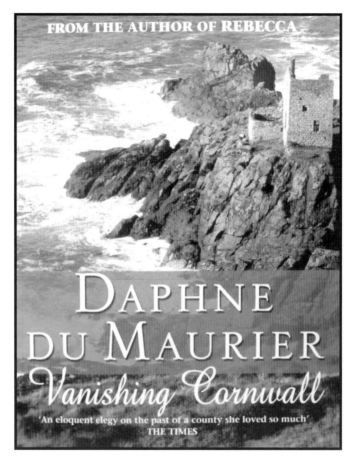

FROM THE AUTHOR OF REBECCA

DAPHNE DU MAURIER
Vanishing Cornwall

'An eloquent elegy on the past of a county she loved so much'
THE TIMES

The cover of Vanishing Cornwall, published by Virago Press in 2007, introduced and with numerous new photographs by Christian Browning. Words and illustrations make this a vital book for Cornwall: a celebration of history, anecdote and travelogue. These 220 pages are a powerful plea for Cornwall's preservation. An earlier edition had been published by Victor Gollancz in 1967.

[Photo: David Flower]

1967 saw a literary collaboration between the two: Daphne's *Vanishing Cornwall* a book about the spirit and history of Cornwall which Kits illustrated. Its dedication, written at Menabilly the year before, reads 'To the memory of my husband, because of memories shared and a mutual love for Cornwall; and to our son Christian who photographed the present, while I rambled on about the past.'

The steady erosion of the Cornish landscape: more buildings, wider roads, the expanding wind mills, yet another camp site, towns and villages spreading. It is, for those who love our countryside and coastline, a depressing situation. How much landscape will be left in 100 years?

In such an environment Daphne's *Vanishing Cornwall* is an important book: a warning in words and pictures. Planners travelling its pages would have to admit they and we are in danger of losing so much heritage.

Daphne's beloved Bodmin Moor is neither sacred nor safe. Oh, for a Lady Sayer to bugle its cause or, better still, the status of a national park.

The 2007 edition of *Vanishing Cornwall*, published by Virago, is a sumptuous production with the bonus of a thoughtful, thought-provoking introduction by Christian Browning. He has taken many new photographs: glorious pictures of locations like the hermit's Roche Rock, Warleggan Church, haunted by the ghost of Rector Densham, Place, that majestic house above Fowey, the castle ruins at Tintagel. And characters like John Wesley, those contrasting Civil War knights, Richard and Bevil Grenville, and Daphne walking alone in the rain.

Daphne, among the family, was known as 'Track.' Here is a paragraph from Christian Browning's introduction: 'Although I'd been brought up at Menabilly from the age of three, I'd never seen much of the county apart from the immediate region around Fowey. School holidays were always taken up with cricket and football, trips to the cinema, picnics at the beach and going on the boat, so my knowledge of the rest of Cornwall was very limited. The next three weeks were magical for me. In the evenings, we would sit by a roaring fire, Track with her whisky and me with my Worthington beer, and she would brief me about the next day's expedition, the places to be visited and the various strange characters that had inhabited them. We loved chatting about the day's events, and she would tell me what she was going to write. We would get endless giggles about some of the more eccentric happenings and it was wonderful to see her beautiful blue eyes filled with tears of laughter.'

*   *   *

Jamaica Inn is a favourite novel for many Cornish readers; Mary Yellan, at the heart of it all, an enduring heroine.

The reluctant debutante, who became the famous novelist, had a gift – genius perhaps – of hooking her readers on the opening page. Her governess encouraged Daphne, constantly telling her she could write. And how well Daphne opens this doom-laden tale – I have an autographed copy alongside as these sentences take shape. Mary travelling across a bleak Bodmin Moor: 'the whole body of the coach trembled and swayed, rocking between the high wheels like a drunken man.'

The Dame's handwriting scarcely changed for many years retaining a distinctive flourish with a pronounced D for Daphne, her typewritten letters coming from an old manual typewriter.

An early photograph of the lounge at Jamaica Inn. Daphne's novel making Jamaica probably the most famous inn in the land. In the older parts at night, when the customers have departed and staff and guests are in their bedrooms, the atmosphere changes, almost like stepping back in time.

*Kathryn Sumner playing the part of Mary Yellan at Truro in 2005. Kathryn said to me
'As a teenager I had read the novel* Jamaica Inn *and was enthralled and here I am playing
Mary in Cornwall, not far from where Daphne du Maurier lived or all that far from the
famous inn. Fantastic'. Many Cornish readers would vote Mary their favourite literary
heroine, another example of Daphne's genius in creating enduring characters.*

Mary Yellan really stars in this dark story of wrecking and high drama along the coast and out on the moor, and in June 2005 I had the luck to be at Hall for Cornwall, Truro, to see Kathryn Sumner play her role in the Salisbury Playhouse's production – a convincing, spirited Mary she made. This piece of theatre incorporating innovative design, music and some original song reminded us, if we needed reminding, how Daphne's stories translate so well on stage or screen. In the case of *Jamaica Inn*, eighteen chapters soaked in murder and mystery.

Who can come to the village of Altarnun and not think of Francis Davey, the villain in dog collar, his hair white under his black shovel hat?

The novel, her first big success, would have thrilled her father. Gerald too would have seen the theatrical possibilities. He was knighted in 1922 for his services to the theatre, recognition for the most distinguished actor-manger of his era. Sir Gerald had created a new naturalistic technique and tone of acting.

Daphne's biography *Gerald, A Portrait* is a remarkable volume, published in 1934 only six months after his death. It was considered 'shocking' by many of his friends and fans but was an enormous breakthrough, earning critical acclaim and really launching her career. Her three earlier novels had been fairly well received but there was no sign of the greatness to come. This was a turning of the tide.

GB Stern reviewing it said 'The chronicle has a queer enchantment. It is the heart-rending story of what we could not but suspect must and would happen to all the Peter Pans who are compelled to grow up and take their places in the material world of grown men and women... The author, you see, has made us care so terribly about the life of Gerald du Maurier.'

Though discreet, Daphne did, in fact, make reference to Gerald's stable of young actresses. Theatre folklore has it that only Gracie Fields turned him down. Margaret Forster, in her riveting introduction to the 2004 Virago edition of the book, referred to Daphne's 'truth between the lines.'

Gerald du Maurier as a young man, before he was knighted. A much loved actor-manager at Wyndham's Theatre, Gerald was the epitome of the matinee idol. His eldest daughter Angela later recalled 'The Theatre was my background from the beginning of time.' While Daphne reckoned her grandfather George du Maurier and her father both had a strange restlessness. J. B. Priestley, who had a spell at Bossiney in North Cornwall during the last war, considered Daphne's biography of her father 'An original and remarkable performance... a flowing, fluid chronicle, an experiment that triumphantly succeeds'.

It was another Virago title that brought me to Fowey in May 2011: *The Doll: Short Stories* a baker's dozen written by Daphne launched at the Daphne du Maurier Festival. Many of these short stories had only recently been discovered, three of them by Ann Willmore, a du Maurier devotee and walking encyclopaedia, who owns a splendid bookshop in Fowey. Also on the platform talking about the new collection were Polly Samson, an acclaimed writer and lyricist, who had written a champagne introduction to the collection, and Professor Helen Taylor of the University of Exeter. A grand occasion culminating in a question and answer session reminiscent of Freddie Grisewood and *Any Questions?* – a golden age of radio.

In her introduction Polly Samson observed 'While considering these stories, I read in Daphne du Maurier's memoir *Myself When Young* that her first kisses, stolen ones with her cousin Geoffrey (twice-married and twenty-two years her senior), reminding her of kissing Gerald... "The strange thing is it's so like kissing D (addy)..." '

There's no doubt Daphne loved her father deeply but not as deeply as he loved her – that realisation came and made her feel uncomfortable. His need for her became a burden. Growing up, she discovered, was not much fun being father's favourite. And she was further perplexed to learn he wished he was not her father, but her brother, and that she was a boy who would never grow up.

This new harvest of stories was great news for the army of du Maurier fans and should introduce her work to a younger readership. Though most were written in Daphne's earlier phases, they reveal her gift of generating atmosphere and tension, a maturity far beyond her years. They reflect too her masterly employment of dialogue, driving plots forward, illuminating character, her principal characters developing, in the reader's imagination, like photographs in the photographer's darkroom.

These thirteen stories remind us of Daphne's biographer Margaret Forster saying "No other writer has so triumphantly defied classification."

Daphne's work has been adapted for radio numerous times; the power of her storytelling means her fiction works well in this medium – and recently the BBC Radio 4 had broadcast some of these tales.

Her son Kits told me: 'She loved writing short stories. They were so different from her novels which she likened to producing a baby, about nine months. She came on holidays abroad with us on a number of occasions and invariably brought a notebook. Something seen, a snippet of conversation heard. She might be enjoying her Dubonnet before lunch and something would catch her attention.

'Though she wasn't religious in a conventional sense, vicars interested her, they made good subjects. I went with her on visits to Warleggan where Densham, this reclusive vicar, made cardboard figures, put them into the pews and preached to them. He was dead but we sensed him pacing the rectory gardens, a sad man, a sad place. But the moor itself is so stimulating... beautiful, mysterious and timeless.

'It was her grandfather, George du Maurier, who inspired Daphne's interest in time travel and what she called dreaming true, in his novel *Peter Ibbetson*. She used the theme of the future and the past in many of her stories.'

A classic example was *The House on the Strand*, shaped when she was living at Kilmarth. Part 'straight' novel, part tale of suspense, it tells of a professor in bio-physics taking a drug and finding himself back in the Cornwall of the 1300s.

Kits and his beautiful wife Hacker, a former model and Miss Eire, live in one of the most celebrated residences in all Cornwall: Ferryside, Bodinnick. Blue and white, and shuttered, it was once the boat builder's yard. The family has resided here for over eighty years.

In the course of a rare interview there, he told me: 'This is an extraordinary collection and we are all deeply indebted to Ann at Bookends. It's incredible to think that my mother wrote a story, like The Doll, at the age of just twenty... she wrote it in this house.

'A doll with mechanical parts in the 1920s. Can you imagine what her mother and father would have said about their daughter writing such a story? And what would Q, a great family friend, have thought about this tale of obsession?'

And it's fascinating that the raven-haired character at the heart of this obsession is called Rebecca.

How a book grows and finds a publisher is sometimes a fascinating story. Conversation with Ann Willmore underlines that fact. Ann is not just an accomplished bookseller. She is an expert, particularly on Cornish books and there is a whiff of Miss Marple about her. She certainly needed those detective attributes. I began by asking her 'How did you find these du Maurier short stories? And what did you do in helping to get them published?'

Ann explained: 'David and I have lived in Fowey, running Bookends of Fowey, for nearly nine years now and through the book shop we work hard to promote authors connected with Cornwall and especially Daphne du Maurier, Sir Arthur Quiller-Couch and AL Rowse. What is less well known is that I have been a collector of Daphne de Maurier for about twenty years, long before we moved to Fowey.

Ann Willmore in Bookends of Fowey, the secondhand bookshop she runs with her husband.

'I've been interested in Daphne du Maurier short stories for a long time and feel they are much overlooked. In my searching I found many of the short stories had been published in magazines in the UK and in the USA during the 1940s, 50s and 60s and started to collect magazines and journals that included her short stories or articles by or about the du Mauriers. I also started looking at books of short stories with contributions by different authors and found that some of Daphne's short stories were published in these collections.'

Ann went on to recall: 'Two other short stories *East Wind* and *The Limpet* were published in collections of du Maurier short stories in the US by Doubleday, but were not included in the UK publications. The manuscript of *East Wind* is in the archives at the University of Exeter, and so we can confirm that it was written in about 1926. *The Limpet* was written much later in about 1958, when Daphne was writing the stories for the collection called *The Breaking Point.* I found them both in American books.

'The fifth story that I found is *The Doll.* Daphne actually mentions writing this in her autobiography *Growing Pains*, so we know she wrote it at Ferryside in January 1928; then it completely disappeared. Knowing that it had to exist I searched many, many times on the internet and eventually a reference came up, a book called *The Editor Regrets* which is a compilation of short stories, by different authors, all of which had been rejected by publishers or magazine editors. The book was edited by George Joseph and published by Michael Joseph in 1937. So there it was after all those years. I had found *The Doll.*

'I confirmed with Kits that none of these five stories had been published in book form in the UK and then asked him if he would take them to the literary agents Curtis Brown to see if they thought it would be possible to publish them. I made up a presentation folder of copies of the five stories from the books and magazines that I had found them in and

Kits took all this to Curtis Brown. Their response was very positive and so the five stories were passed on to Virago who also showed an interest. Virago felt that five stories were not enough, so they added eight stories from the collection called Early Stories, which had not been in print since the 1950s.

'Quite quickly I discovered that the same short story could appear with a different title so, for example, I might find a publication including the story *Mazie,* only to discover that this story is also called London. Eventually, however, I did find two stories in magazines which I had never seen before anywhere. The first one was *And His Letters Grew Colder*, which was in an American magazine called *Hearst's International* combined with *Cosmopolitan,* dated September 1931.

'This short story was included in *The du Maurier Companion* edited by Professor Helen Taylor and published in 2007 to celebrate Daphne's centenary. There is no information to say when or where Daphne wrote this story, but it has to be about 1928, because it closely follows the theme of other short stories written at that time. The second story is called *The Happy Valley* and was published in *The Illustrated London News* in the Christmas 1932 edition: there's no trace of this story anywhere else. It's particularly interesting because much of it is set in the grounds of Menabilly and the happy valley of the title is the same as the one referred to later on in *Rebecca*. This story has to have been written after Daphne started trespassing in the grounds of Menabilly (around 1926-29) and found the house, because that is woven into the plot.'

The Doll – Kits's favourite story in this 2011 collection – is an incredible piece of writing. We find ourselves wondering about those sodden discoloured pages in that shabby pocket book and trying to locate the nameless bay, surely not far from Fowey. We are hooked – hooked for the next seventeen pages.

I too am drawn to vicars in life and fiction and therefore savoured every line of *And Now to God the Father:* a vain London parson, a man with ambition who preaches one set of rules from his pulpit on Sunday and lives by another set from Monday to Saturday. Is he perhaps the literary ancestor of Francis Davey in *Jamaica Inn*?

It was, of course, a real vicar of Altarnun who sowed the seeds of that novel, launched in 1936 with the publisher's warning 'Don't start this book if you're alone in the house at night, with the wind howling outside...'

A lot of Daphne's ideas for novels and short stories came through carefully observing people. As she once put it: 'Often a story would well up in my mind but would take a long time to mature.' She knew when the moment was right to sit in front of her typewriter and turn those ideas into words, sentences and paragraphs. A writer who relished the challenge and discipline of constructing a short story.

Anyone, wanting to know about the family background, would do well to read Daphne's *The du Mauriers*. Originally published in 1937, she tells the story from the departure from England to France in 1810 of Mary Anne Clarke, mistress of the Duke of York and the author's great-great-grandmother, to 1863 and 'Kicky' (George du Maurier) her grandfather marrying. There's a fascinating family tree at the back of the book and in her dedication at the front Daphne wrote 'In the belief that there are thirty-one descendants of Louis-Mathurin Busson du Maurier and his wife Ellen Jocelyn Clarke alive today, the story of the past is dedicated to all of them, with affection. October 1936.'

An interesting fact of literary life is that the Westcountry has produced two immensely successful women writers: both Dames, Daphne and Agatha Christie across the Tamar in Devon. There is another parallel, both dominated by their houses. Agatha, the author of more than eighty detective stories, was held by Ashfield in Torquay, where she was born and brought up, until she was fifty. Then there was her adored Greenway on the River Dart which she called 'the loveliest house in the world.' They admired one another's work but never met. What a meeting that would have been.

There are many lovely books in my library but there is no doubt about the most beautifully produced. It has to be Daphne du Maurier's *Classics of the Macabre*, number 10 in a limited edition of 200 signed by the author and the illustrator Michael Foreman whose artistry adds to the eerie atmosphere running through these six long short stories.

It's surprising that this collection, which takes us to the very edge of the unknown, should have been written by someone who was 'not at all psychic – I have never seen a ghost or dabbled in spiritualism or the occult – I have always been fascinated by the unexplained, the darker side of life.' Knowing my own paranormal interest, she said she had no doubt some people saw ghosts and believed they may have been fragments of film from the past. Now to the value of Daphne's books. Ann Willmore of Bookends has these considered thoughts:

'There are a number of special titles: *The Loving Spirit*, UK first edition, published by William Heinemann in 1931. This seldom comes along in a dustwrapper, but one did sell at auction two years go for just under £2000. Without dustwrapper it is still very scarce and a very good copy could be worth £600 - £700.

'*Jamaica Inn*, UK first edition in dustwrapper and in very good condition, published by Victor Gollancz in 1936 - value £5000, but if signed could sell for as much as £10,000 - £15,000. *Jamaica Inn* is actually a rarer book than *Rebecca* and so can command slightly higher prices.

'*Rebecca*, UK first edition, in dustwrapper and in very good condition, published by Victor Gollancz in 1938 – value £5000, but if signed could have a value of £10,000.

'There are copies of both *Jamaica Inn* and *Rebecca* which have suffered over the years and so being in less good condition the price comes down a lot. I recently sold a signed first edition *Rebecca* without dustwrapper for £1000, because its covers were somewhat marked and faded and there was foxing throughout the book, and, of course no dustwrapper, so all these things reduced the value.

'*The Apple Tree*, UK first edition, in dustwrapper and in very good condition, published by Victor Gollancz in 1952 is £150 - £200. Signed copies are incredibly scarce, so I would estimate their value at £500 - £1000. This book is important because it is where the short story of *The Birds* appears for the first time.

'Other titles with high values would include *I'll Never Be Young Again*, *The Progress of Julius*, *Frenchman's Creek* and *My Cousin Rachel*, all of which would be valued at £100 - £250 for a

very good UK first edition in dustwrapper, increasing to £800 - £1000 for a signed copy. First editions in dustwrappers of Daphne's other titles would be valued at £25 - £75, with signed copies valued at £200 - £400.'

In 1993 there was an impressive sequel to *Rebecca* when Susan Hill's *Mrs de Winter* was published. Some people may say the novel does not need a follow-up but the fact is it does leave all sorts of unanswered questions. Is Maxim truly off the hook? How are his finances – can Manderley be rebuilt? And what lies ahead for the nameless second wife? Does the ghost of Rebecca continue to haunt her?

As for the choice of Susan Hill, Antony Harwood, director at Curtis Brown, the literary agency which handles the du Maurier estate, said 'It was not really a question of choosing her. It was whether Susan Hill would do a sequel because everything in her writing matches perfectly with du Maurier's and particularly Rebecca.' Press reports say that Susan Hill, who loves cricket, was paid £1,000,000 to write the book.

I greatly enjoyed a later sequel: Sally Beauman's *Rebecca's Tale*, launched in 2001. Joanna Trollope, reviewing it, declared 'Passionate, vivid, elusive... as compelling as the original. A real achievement.' It is quite simply the book for any du Maurier reader who ever dreamt of going back to Manderley again.

A du Maurier legacy is the annual Festival that bears her name, devoted to literature and the arts. It has brought a host of famous names to Fowey, the 2011 programme included Sir Tim Rice, lyricist and broadcaster, cricketer and author; John Sergeant, the former BBC chief political correspondent and an unforgettable *Strictly Come Dancing* competitor; the Irish folk singer Cara Dillon and larger than life politician Anne Widdecombe, another ballroom performer. The Festival's continuation is important for Cornwall.

You cannot profile Daphne du Maurier and not mention her relationship with Gertrude Lawrence, which, for a time, enriched her life and gave verve to her writing.

'Gertie was more than a brilliant actress. She was ravishing. I'm not surprised Daphne fell for her.' That was the opinion of Derek Tangye who was in MI5 during the war and whose wife Jean was Public Relations Officer for The Savoy and Claridge's for a decade. 'Gertie was ageless. So full of fun and life.'

The fact that Gertrude Lawrence starred in Daphne's play *September Tide* in London added to the magnetism. Curiously or perhaps not so curiously she had been Gerald's last actress love. She was ten years older than Daphne, and their relationship is a reminder that the author's passionate, violent stories sometimes mirrored her own inner life – the line between reality and fantasy slender.

The 1980s were tragic years for Daphne: her writing gifts gone, her memory poor, though she did not suffer from Alzheimer's disease. Close Cornish friends like Clara Vyvyan and Foy Quiller-Couch had departed this life.

Esther Rowe very kindly arranged that I should see her at Kilmarth. She signed a couple of books but she didn't know me and, even worse, when I told her I had recently been in Penzance and seen the house in Chapel Street with its Bronte links, she looked blank. She then turned to Esther and asked 'Did I write about the Brontes?' The meeting was painfully short as she retreated behind her newspaper.

She died in April 1989. Esther Rowe, who gave her devoted service, was convinced Lady Browning (as she called her) was willing herself to death. It was Esther who, taking breakfast to her bedroom, found the light still on. She had died in her sleep.

Kilmarth, the dower house of Menabilly, about four furlongs away: Daphne's final Cornish home. Her housekeeper, Esther Rowe, lived in a cottage next door. One of the last occasions I saw Daphne was in the grounds of Kilmarth when Tamsin Thomas and I were making a series for BBC Radio Cornwall on locations in du Maurier territory. Today Kilmarth is a private residence and not open to the public - as is Menabilly.

Bringing this portrait to a close is difficult. My very last memory of Daphne was seeing her looking so frail yet striding along a path, her nurse companion some twenty paces behind and her dog scampering ahead. Or reading a favourite novel *My Cousin Rachel*, her last historical novel set in Cornwall, with its Jane Eyre atmosphere.

The stage version was further evidence of Daphne's class, the writing convincingly beautiful about women as well as men, Rachel coming across as a mysterious character. We could argue for hours about her true motives. Kits Browning recently said to me 'Mother liked to tease her readers,' and there may be something of that is in this 1951 novel.

It was a visit to Antony House in south east Cornwall that triggered her idea: the portrait of Rachel Carew inspiring. I think it still hangs in the porch room at Antony. There is an important difference between the real Rachel Carew and Daphne's Rachel in that Miss Carew married Ambrose Manaton of Kilworthy and died tragically young.

When a notable figure – like a bestselling novelist and a Dame of the British Empire – dies, it is often said 'a light has gone out.' But Daphne will never die. She lives on in her stories and in our imagination.

Angela in her early 30s: the most social of the three sisters. Friends meant a good deal to her: 'Most of the friendships I formed when I was young I have kept,' she wrote in Old Maids Remember. 'A girl at school; various people whom one met and became attached to when they were acting with my father; a man or woman met by chance at a party, which started a '"something"'and has lasted.' Her admiration of horses is reflected in the fact that hunters at the Royal Cornwall Show at Wadebridge annually compete for her cup. Music was another of her loves and she admitted that if she were a music snob it was because she wanted to hear 'the best artistes'. And she came to enjoy the Royal Ballet nearly as much as opera - as a child she had been kissed by Pavlova.

ANGELA

A live or dead,' said Angela du Maurier, 'I must be near water.'

She is buried in the peaceful churchyard of St Winnow, about three miles up river from Ferryside. It is hard to imagine a more beautiful church location: the curve of the river, the woods of Ethy, sloping green fields, gulls calling. The scenery and the atmosphere are essentially south Cornish. This church was the setting for the wedding between Dwight Enys and Caroline Penvenen in the BBC *Poldark* TV series.

In the eye of imagination too we can see Sir Arthur Quiller-Couch and his daughter Foy Felicia rowing by, fascinated by the linking of Fowey River and the Tristan and Iseult legend. Or Angela herself coming here for church services. The actor Eric Portman is buried at St Veep. An area which encourages curiosity.

There is something not easily defined about St Winnow church and churchyard, a serenity, an almost timeless quality, all wrapped up with centuries of living and worshiping. The church we see today stood on the same land where the Oratory of St Winnoc was probably erected at the end of the 600s. Nothing remains of that building. It would have been cob - mud and straw - with reed.

The church coincided with the arrival of the Normans, the construction beginning about the twelfth century. As for St Winnoc, he was a Celtic priest and evangelist, one of that army of holy characters who extended the Christian faith after the departure of the Romans.

Angela always gave the impression of being in a hurry. The only time she was likely to linger was when she was enjoying a Cinzano. Angela wrote ten works of fiction, two volumes of autobiography and *Pilgrims By The Way*, a journey to the Holy Land.

The vicar of her parish had said to her one is never quite the same person having been to Jerusalem... 'At the time I did not take in his remark, it was the sort of thing any parson would probably feel. I know differently now.'

A high Anglican, Angela was 97 when she died in February 2002 and all through her life, she remained true to high church ritual and teaching. Churches, in fact, played a big part in her love of Cornwall. Moreover she did more than her share in helping them, opening fetes to raise money for these lovely old buildings. She had special affection for two other churches in the area: Bodinnick's small St John's was dear to her because it was converted from an old stable, and Lanteglos-by-Fowey. In her chapter in *My Cornwall*, published in 1973, she wrote of Lanteglos: 'At Christmas we have midnight Mass there when the church is lit by candles, candles in the window sills, candles in the pews, many candles on the altar. I go with two friends every year to prepare and light them.'

Angela experienced bad luck in that when Michael Joseph launched her first novel *The Perplexed Heart* in 1939, the year that war began; it was soon after Daphne's successful Cornish classic *Jamaica Inn*, and in the wake of the phenomenal *Rebecca*. Angela knew, in her heart, she could not compete.

She was further unfortunate in that her first manuscript had been rejected on the grounds that it had a lesbian theme. There had been furore over Radclyffe Hall's *The Well of Loneliness*, also a lesbian subject, and publishers were nervous. *The Little Less* did, in fact, see the light of publication in 1941. It's rumoured Daphne regarded this title 'an unsuitable read' for her children's nanny. If this novel had launched her career, then she would have hit the headlines and won serious literary criticism.

Wallace Nichols, the literary allrounder from West Cornwall who, in his London years, had read manuscripts and edited, told me in an interview in the 1960s:

'*Treveryan* is a strong novel, as Gothic as anything written by Daphne. Treveryan, like Manderley in *Rebecca*, is the dominant character and Angela is especially good on relationships.' But he believed *The Little Less* should have been accepted earlier as a manuscript. 'As a publisher's reader I would have recommended it for publication. It would have made a big difference to her career.'

Just supposing there had been no Daphne, would Angela have emerged as a more famous author? Some say Angela did not have her sister's imagination for fiction. That may be true but others believed Angela could and should have written more. When Daphne read *My Cornwall* she rated Angela's chapter 'Excellent... she should write more things like that.'

Soon after I lunched with her friend Lady Clara Vyvyan at her historic home Trelowarren down on the Lizard peninsula and she agreed: 'The problem is Angela does so many other things. The theatre and the dogs, the church and her politics and her friends. These are all important to her.'

Although overshadowed by her younger sister, Angela showed no resentment, the sisters remaining devoted to one another.

The one area in which Angela surpassed Daphne was in autobiographical writing - more amusing, more honest. It is significant though that she called her first volume *It's Only The Sister*. Nevertheless her memoirs won some golden assessments.

Here is *The Western Mail* reviewing *Old Maids Remember*:

> 'Miss du Maurier is a strong personality with decided and strong opinions. She can even provoke one to arguing out loud with the book, triumphantly creating a conversation instead of a monologue.'

A great traveller, she once reflected 'To fall in love with a place is as exciting as to fall in love with a human being. I have done both and often.' She never married.

Margaret Forster, writing her obituary in *The Independent*, said she was annoyed by people who thought spinsters, like herself, knew little about sex and love. 'She recounted how from the age of six to 25 she had fallen in love repeatedly "without a trace of love coming into it" but that later she thought it foolish "to live in ignorance of one of life's pleasures... to be as white as the driven snow at 30 is just damn silly." Angela, it must be assumed, was proud of not having been silly.'

Angela du Maurier and I shared an interest in alternative medicine, both believers in the power of spiritual healing. She had a dog which had lost all his fur. 'He was as bare as a tiny elephant,' as she put it.

One day, she came across the details of an animal sanctuary which did 'absent healing.' So she sent the dog's details and 'a little while later his hair began to sprout.' And Angela was convinced another sick dog Cleo was helped by prayers from the same sanctuary.

She recalled too that a beautiful race horse, Tulyar, a Derby winner no less, won her some money. Then Tulyar was sold to an American owner but succumbed to a strange illness. Angela could not bear the thought of such a noble equine being put down – so again she sent details to the sanctuary. About a year later she read in a Sunday newspaper of the animal's 'miraculous recovery.'

It so happened that a Westcountry spiritual healer approached me about the possibility of writing a book for a national publisher. I knew she had achieved some remarkable results with animals and birds but equally I knew she sadly lacked the ability to write a good enough manuscript. So I asked Angela for her thoughts on the problem.

Her response was positive and encouraging: 'If her stories are strong enough, a publisher will probably use a professional to help with rewriting.'

Angela went on to recall 'When Michael Joseph accepted *The Perplexed Heart*, my first published novel, we spent hours going through the manuscript, generally taking things out. I became so despondent I asked him why he'd bothered to publish it. He generously replied "Because I believe you'll go on to write really good books."'

I probably knew Angela du Maurier best through animal welfare. Her concern for the cause went deeper than sending a cheque or an autographed book to a fund-raising event. She felt strongly about the practical side of animal welfare.

Angela loved dogs. She was therefore interested in rescue work and had ideals on the subject considering it important to match the animal to its new owner. She also felt a checking system necessary whereby animals were seen in their new environment – and that all was well. In her London years, she had been the RSPCA secretary for Hampstead and had walked miles, from house to house, with her tins collecting money for the Society.

She also believed food animals should not be exported live for the dinner table in other countries. She loathed the idea of sheep being transported from Cornwall to say Italy, and was firmly committed to the cause that no British horses, ponies or donkeys should be exported for 'horse meat' in Europe.

Angela though did surprise some of her animal welfare friends by supporting fox hunting. She believed foxes had to be controlled, and that hunting was effective and part of countryside tradition.

Angela du Maurier's love of Bodinnick and Fowey and the surrounding district leads us to ask this question: 'Why has the area attracted so many writers and motived so many books?'

Sir Arthur Quiller-Couch, Kenneth Grahame, Leo Warmsley, Denys Val Baker and Tim Heald are only some of the authors who have found inspiration hereabouts and interestingly an eminent presentday painter, like John Brenton, son of china clay territory, has painted some beautiful images in oils, around Fowey and Polruan.

'Writers are inclined to follow paths which lead on to remote places and they look for beauty and a degree of solitude.' That's the view of Rachael Smith-Rawnsley, a former publisher's editor who now works at Wyndhams, Sir Gerald du Maurier's old London theatre. At one point Rachael had a year at Fowey working in the local museum and she added 'Fowey is a port of moods. One day you think you're in the south of France and another it's essentially Cornwall and so Cornish. Fowey's moody in that the atmosphere changes. I remember a grey misty morning when the police were looking for the bodies of two young people who had drowned out rowing. I think too of shipwrecks. And other days you have this brilliant light giving colour and form, an environment that appeals naturally to writers and painters.'

And the value of Angela's books? Ann Willmore has come up with some interesting facts and figures.

'Angela du Maurier's books tend to be less easy to find than Daphne's,' she said. 'There are four titles which stand out.

'Very good copies in dustwrapper of *It's Only the Sister*, UK first edition, published by Peter Davies in 1951 and *Old Maids Remember*, UK first edition, published by Peter Davies in 1966 would both have values of about £80-£100. Signed copies would be worth about £150-£200.

'*Birkinshaw and Other Stories*, UK first edition in dustwrapper, published by Peter Davies in 1948 is a very scarce book indeed. It is valued at about £150, but a signed copy would be valued at about £300-£400.

'*The Little Less* is Angela's famous lesbian novel and so commands particular interest. UK first editions published by Peter Davies in 1941 are almost impossible to find. A very good copy in dustwrapper would be about £200 and a signed copy about £350-£400.

'As you can see Angela's books command comparatively high prices, but her signature does not add a tremendous amount to the value, unlike Daphne.'

A boost came for Angela in 2003 when Truran, the Cornish publishers, brought back into circulation three of her titles: her memoirs *It's Only the Sister* and two novels *The Road to Leenane* and *Treveryan*. The first novel, reflecting her love of Ireland, captures the vanished kingdom of high Irish morals and romance. It's the story of a Catholic woman tormented by her love for a married man. The second, in the words of Sally Beauman is about 'strong women and weak men, an abiding love that breaks taboos, and dares not be declared.' It is dedicated 'with much Love to my sister Daphne.' Sonia and I had the pleasure of attending the launching of all three titles at Ferryside: a memorable morning in the very heart of du Maurier Country – a splendid hat-trick.

*   *   *

A grey wet December day but four magpies hovering, though gulls flying across the valley suggest rough weather to come. The perfect day to read a good book and I'm deep into *Old Maids Remember*, published by Peter Davies in 1966.

The idea came to Angela travelling on the railway, bound for a wedding in Dublin. We can hear her distinctive voice as we travel through this alphabet of memories: a whiff of the Headmistress when she spoke conjuring up images of Celia Johnston, that formidable lady in *The Prime of Miss Jean Brodie*. It was while Angela was lying in her bath one day that the alphabet slowly grew.

Her family inevitably features strongly: 'P is for parents' and 'S is for Sisters.' Her father turns up again: 'T is for Theatre.' There's humour, notably in 'O is for Operations.' A bonus to this copy is that a previous owner has enclosed a magazine photograph cutting of the Mitford Sisters in the 1930s: Jessica, Nancy, Diana, Unity and Pamela. Like the du Mauriers, they had a powerful sense of family, their niece Lady Emma Tennant saying 'When I think of my aunts, I think of gales of laughter.'

As for the du Maurier girls we visualise them playing cricket on the lawn. Daphne and Angela sharing secrets and their mother complaining 'You always stick up for each other.' This is a volume we relish like enjoying a stylish claret, Angela producing something startling, even sparkling, under seemingly innocuous topics. It is dedicated to the memory of her friend Naomi Jacob and Angela begins her dedication: 'Micky darling, you were always asking for a second instalment of *Only the Sister*, and when I saw you - for the last time - I told you I had begun *Old Maids Remember*, and it's for you.'

And there is a reference to sisters in the S chapter that fits this publication like a quality pair of gloves from Simpsons in London or Simpsons in Penzance. Here is a fragment:

'I suppose all our interests are fairly diverse, but as there are only three miles and a river between Daphne and me, we see each other a great deal oftener than either of us see Jeanne, who lives in Devon with a friend, and has five horses, seven dogs, five goats, a cat, birds, poultry, pigeons, heaven knows how many acres of ground as well as her thatched house. All three of us are good letter writers...'

What a fascinating book such letters would have made.

And in a way *Old Maids Remember* is the next best thing to a letter from Angela du Maurier. She takes us into her confidence. In places it is as if she takes us to one side and says 'Now there's something I want to tell you.'

Angela du Maurier with Westcountry author and journalist Sarah Foot in the garden at Ferryside in the late 1970s when Sarah, a member of the famous Foot family, was researching her book Following the River Fowey. *In it she wrote 'Over the years the du Maurier family has modernised the house but left all its old magic'. Sarah recalled Angela telling her the three sisters and their mother had immediately fallen in love with the property and Gerald du Maurier bought it within three days.*

There are fourteen grand old black and white photographs among these 190 pages and fittingly the frontispiece of Angela is the most striking, a furrowed brow perhaps but every inch the air of an aristocrat, a picture worth a thousand words.

And here is how she ends it: 'By the time this is published – if it ever is – that bridegroom in Dublin will be the father of a boy or girl, and I shall be sixty-one. That alphabet is finished, the song is ended.'

*   *   *

I am back at Angela's grave in St Winnow churchyard wondering if there is perhaps one episode that sums her up – on reflection it has to be the afternoon when the Queen and Prince Philip visited Menabilly.

Daphne was anxious about entertaining the monarch at the mansion. Would everything be in order? She needlessly worried about etiquette. Fourteen gathered for afternoon tea, produced by Esther Rowe, Daphne's housekeeper.

But Daphne found confidence from Angela's presence who chatted comfortably, easily with the Royal visitors, Angela proving she was the most assured of the three sisters, an hour and a half she would never have forgotten.

Jeanne du Maurier, the painter: St Ives was an important chapter in her life, her development as a painter at a time when there was conflict between the old school artists and the modern movement. Jeanne went to live on Dartmoor, an area she grew to love deeply, responding to the power in the landscape. Like Frederick John Widgery before her, she found creative impulse here.

JEANNE

Born in 1911, Jeanne was the youngest of the du Maurier sisters and, like her grandfather George, she chose to become a painter. So when the family came to their Cornish home in 1926, Jeanne's motivation sharpened.

On a good day, there is luminous light and variety always: countryside and coastline, modest cottages and majestic properties like Place, home of the Treffrys, and, above all, the River Fowey flowing into the Channel.

Jeanne studied at the Central School of Art in Southampton Row where she was in the life class under Bernard Meninsky; she also studied drypoint and etching there. Later she went on to the St John's Wood School of Art, studying painting under the tutelage of PF Millard. Her first studio was in Hampstead and in 1938 she began exhibiting in public.

Following the death of her father and the start of the war in 1939, the family moved permanently to Ferryside, and for the duration Jeanne stopped painting to concentrate on operating a market garden, with Angela, distributing foodstuffs locally and sending some upcountry.

In the autumn of 1945 Jeanne had an exhibition, opened by her mother Lady du Maurier, the actress Muriel Beaumont.

When peace returned, Jeanne resumed painting, revealing a growing sense of colour and outline – and assurance. She took a studio in St Ives where she met Dod Proctor, well-known West Cornwall painter who achieved fame, even notoriety, for her female nude studies. Jeanne and Dod became close friends, spending three winters together: two in Tenerife, and one in Africa.

It was in 1948 that they had met up with Noel Welch, a poet and writer, who was destined to share Jeanne's future home in Devon. A legacy of their tour was a painting *Jeanne's Door* by Dod, shown at the Royal Academy that year.

In St Ives, haunt of artists since J. M. W. Turner, Jeanne found a civil war simmering between the old school painters and the modern movement. She was in sympathy with the revolutionaries and delighted to be made a member of the Penwith Society, the break-away group, which included Barbara Hepworth, Ben Nicholson and Bernard Leach.

In her St Ives years she also became friends with another distinguished painter Alethea Garstin who lived and painted at Zennor. Alethea too was in tune with the modern painters.

A curious fact is Jeanne was dressed as a boy until she was twelve years old and one of her cherished childhood possessions was a box of lead soldiers.

Like Angela she developed a love of dogs, particularly Pekinese.

The girls' mother, Lady Muriel du Maurier, at Ferryside in August 1946. Gerald met her when she was Muriel Beaumont, an actress in J. M. Barrie's The Admirable Crichton in 1902. She gave up acting before the birth of her daughter Jeanne and thereafter devoted herself to Gerald and the family. Claire Wolferstan, a relation of hers and a dear friend of mine interested in the paranormal, said Muriel had no regrets about leaving the stage. In Claire's view 'Muriel would have become a very accomplished actress if she had sustained her career'. Instead she became the perfect hostess at Gerald's many social gatherings.

Jeanne also had a liking for fast cars, a characteristic shared with her nephew Kits who recalls 'An elite sports car, a Daimler Dart, which she drove at a furious pace around those narrow Dartmoor roads and lanes. We often compared notes about our cars.' And when Daphne was researching her glass-blowing ancestors, Jeanne drove her and Noel across du Maurier territory in France.

Noel did, in fact, write a poem *Still Life: Studio Tables*, about one of her paintings. Denys Val Baker published it in the spring edition of *The Cornish Review* in 1972, poetry with echoes of 'the singing colour,' the reflective nature in so much of Jeanne's art.

A painter who remembers Jeanne in her years at Newlyn and St Ives is Margo Maeckelberghe, one of our finest modern painters, a Cornish Bard and the Chairman of the Penwith Society.

'We met several times,' Margo recalled when we talked at her home on the outskirts of Penzance, 'and on one occasion we were fellow exhibitors in a team show in Brittany. Jeanne worked well in both landscapes and interiors... she had a very sure sense of colour and line.

'I remember too seeing a quite famous photograph of three du Mauriers: Lady du Maurier flanked by two of her daughters Jeanne and Daphne... there was a dog too in the picture. It was a long time ago but I think I saw it on a visit to London at the National Portrait Gallery.'

But by the time she exhibited at the Royal Academy in the 1950s, Jeanne had moved to Manaton on Dartmoor. An essentially private person, she worked away quietly at her art and enjoyed the company of Noel.

We met only twice and on both occasions she expressed her appreciation of moorland. Jeanne clearly loved the landscape of Dartmoor and riding across it. I had recently visited Lady Sylvia Sayer and you recognised the passion they both had for wilderness. You thought too of her sister Daphne's attunement with Bodmin Moor, smaller of course but a kindred spirit. Both places firing imagination and speculation. I learned too of Jeanne's pleasure in drinking wine: 'My French ancestry...'

Jeanne was the most selective of the trio. Like Derek Tangye, the Cornish author and countryside philosopher, she took pleasure in quite simple things like a bowl of fruit or a wine bottle. *Half Moon* had a rather bare appearance when you thought of Menabilly or Kilmarth. Some people considered she resembled her father and there was a portrait of Gerald by Augustus John in the hall.

On that first visit we enjoyed a golden sunlit day and, like all painters, she had a keen interest in weather. On such a day you could see why Dartmoor held such an attraction, the beautiful shades and those wide moorland skies.

She was a member of the Newlyn Society of Artists and the Royal West of England Academy. She had a one-woman exhibition in Oxford opened by Dame Ninette de Valois and another in London at the Beaux Arts which the Queen honoured with her presence.

And what does Nicholas St John Rosse of Trethevy make of our Jeanne du Maurier painting. Nicholas, who studied under the great Annigoni, is in the classic mould. He was thoughtful for a while. 'There's a strong sense of geometry,' he said, 'in the door and the wall beyond. The bar on the left of the French window is going straight down through the flower pot and up the garden path and straight through the wall beyond. A psychologist would make something of that. I would have painted a figure of someone disappearing

Jeanne du Maurier's painting of the garden view from inside Half Moon, the house on Dartmoor she shared with Noel Welch. On our first visit, Jeanne gave an impromptu piano performance. Soon the room and seemingly the whole house was filled with Debussy's Clair de Lune. Jeanne striking the keys with remarkable vigour and skill, suddenly becoming twenty-five years younger, an extraordinary transformation. We later noticed this almost completed painting and both liked the work. Jeanne explained she hoped to finish it soon and she would then send it to a gallery. We said we'd be interested in buying it and she was delighted. A price immediately agreed, I collected it later in the month.
[Photo: David Flower]

through the gap in the wall but then I'm a figure painter. It's a painting full of rectangles, a painting that makes you look and think. You asked if it were an oil painting. It is, but it's not been varnished. Many of the moderns don't care for varnish. I do because it gives a certain richness and preserves the art.'

Jeanne was doubtless saddened that her father did not live to see her maturing as a painter. As a girl her black and white drawing demonstrated inherited excellence from her grandfather but she did not begin serious painting during Sir Gerald's life. He had invested in her tennis coaching. Did he expect to see his youngest daughter playing at Wimbledon?

The only sister never to have written a book, you get the impression Jeanne did, in fact, have the material and a literary ally in Noel Welch. But alas no volume emerged. Instead she concentrated on her painting.

Jeanne du Maurier remained the most elusive of the three sisters. Margo Maeckleberghe probably spoke for many when she said 'An interesting woman... one would like to have known her better.'

ABOUT THE AUTHOR

Michael Williams is a Cornishman and Cornish Bard. He and his wife Sonia founded Bossiney Books and were regional publishers for twenty-five years. They live near St Teath,

North Cornwall. Michael's recent authorship includes *Ghosts Around Bodmin Moor* and *Writers in Cornwall*. He is President of Paranormal Investigation, a group exploring the edge of the unknown in the south west, and is currently researching and writing about strange happenings in Cornwall.

Michael is President of the Cornish Crusaders Cricket Club and a Patron of the Broomfield Horse Sanctuary near St Just-in-Penwith. He is also a Patron of Animals Voice and campaigns nationally on animal welfare issues. Over the years he has broadcast on subjects as diverse as King Arthur and Dartmoor, cricket and folklore.

Michael Williams, pictured above with Rachael Smith-Rawnsley and her dog Ruby at The Hurlers stone circles near Minions in 2002. Daphne du Maurier really discovered Bodmin Moor as a young woman when she went on a riding excursion with Foy Quiller-Couch. They stayed at Jamaica Inn, then a temperance house, and entertained the Vicar of Altarnun to supper by a peat fire – the seeds of her great novel were sown. All three sisters owned dogs and responded to dramatic landscape.